Amazon Echo Show

2018 Updated Advanced User Guide to Amazon Echo Show with Step-by-Step Instructions (alexa, dot, echo user guide, echo amazon, amazon dot, echo show, user manual)

ANDREW HOWARD

CONTENTS

Introduction

This book is intended to help users take their use of the Echo Show to another level. This book is setup to help you not only get a clear understanding of what your Echo Show can do but also provide instructions for areas which you may not be familiar with. Feel free to navigate to chapters which peak your interest the most or read the book in one sitting. No matter how you choose to read this book you will receive a plethora of information.

The Amazon Echo Show was one of Amazon's first voice activated assistants with a screen. Not only can it speak information back to you, it can show you. This device is a small power house which boasts a growing list of functionalities.

- Voice & Video calling

- Game play

- Smart home control

- Voice control of music and various other media

The items listed above are only a small subset of what the Amazon Echo show can do. The Echo show will compliment your busy lifestyle by automating the mundane tasks of your day. Checking the weather, checking the time, checking your account balances and even creating to do lists has never been easier using your device.

The purpose of this book is to aid you in navigating not only the obvious features but the hidden gems as well. This book will provide you with all the information needed in order to not just use the basic function but the advanced features as well. Once you have finished this book and set it up to your desired specifications you will only want more devices to aid you in making your life easier. This guide will work with you from the unboxing of your device and forward.

Chapter 1: A Brief Introduction to Your Amazon Echo Show – What It Can Do for You

The Echo Show is a voice activated smart assistant with a 7" touchscreen display. It boasts a completely unique design than the cylindrical style that many are used to. The Echo Show has a boxy angled design with a small camera on the top and 2 speakers on the bottom. The Echo Show is also equipped with 8 microphones around the top of the device. Alexa is the brains and powerhouse of the device. She continues to grow and evolve with time.

What's in the box?

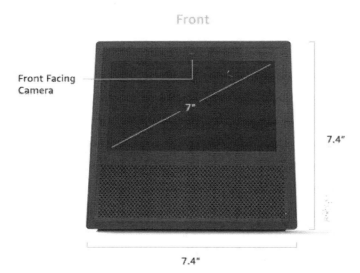

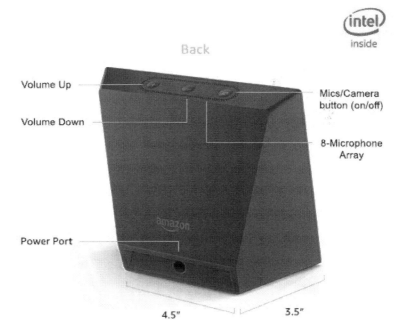

Upon opening your device, don't expect extravagant packaging or too many bells and whistles. There are 4 things included in the box, these include:

- The Echo Show
- Things to try card
- Quick Start Guide
- Power Adapter (6ft)

After you have unboxed your device, you are now ready to begin setup. You can start setup by simply plugging in your Echo Show device and letting it load.

Once you have connected the device you will need to download the Alexa mobile application to continue setup. If you do not have a cellular device available, setup can begin using a computer. This can be done at alexa.amazon.com. Downloading the application allows you to control functions of Alexa with your phone.

Once your device has loaded you will be prompted to connect to your Wi-Fi network on the Echo Show's screen. From the device, you will need to enter in the connectivity information and log into your desired Amazon account. Your device will check for any software updates and install them as needed.

Before completing setup, you will see a short video on basic capabilities with the Echo Show. Once this video is done, your device is ready to go.

Simple to Set Up & Use

| 1. Plug in Echo Show | 2. Connect to the internet using Echo Show | 3. Just ask for music, weather, news, and more |

What do the colors on your device mean?

Your Echo show will use colors as visual cues to communicate its status. These colors will range from Blue to even purple, each having a different meaning. The list below will aid you in understanding what each color means and how it pertains to your Echo Show.

Blue – Blue will appear on your screen after you have used your wake word. This means that Alexa is process your request.

Orange – If your device is glowing orange, there is an issue with your wireless connectivity. Troubleshoot your Wi-Fi and attempt to reconnect.

Purple – This means that the "Do Not Disturb" Feature is currently active.

Red – This color indicates that your camera and mic have been turned off. This can easily be turned back on sing the buttons on the top of the device.

Navigating the Echo Show

Being that your device has a screen, it can be navigated using your voice or its touch features. To navigate back to the home screen simply say, "Alexa, Go Home" or swipe downward from the top of your device and select the home button.

If you are attempting to scroll on your device although you still can say things like, "Alexa, scroll down" it may be easier to swipe the screen. Your screen can be swiped up, down left or right.

Navigating to your settings is also a breeze. You can either tell Alexa to go to your settings for you or swipe downward from the top of the screen and select "Settings". Media playback should be one of the easiest things to do with your device. While listening or watching a specific item you can easily touch the features on the screen. When using Alexa, the following commands can be used:

- "Alexa, rewind"
- "Alexa, forward"
- "Alexa, pause"
- "Alexa, go back"

Optimizing Alexa For Your Voice

Wouldn't it be nice if Alexa could recognize your voice no matter who was talker to her? Wouldn't it be nice if she just knew what to share based on who was talking to her? Now she can do just that. Alexa can now offer personalized results based on who is talking to her.

To set up voice recognition you will need to use your mobile device. Inside of the Alexa application navigate to the "Settings" area. Once there you will need to go through the voice training. Alexa will have you repeat 10 phrases. This should be done with little to no background noise.

Voice training will be quick and easy. Once complete, say the phrase, "Alexa, who am I?". If she responds your training was a success. However, it may take Alexa 15 – 20 to be able to answer who you are accurately.

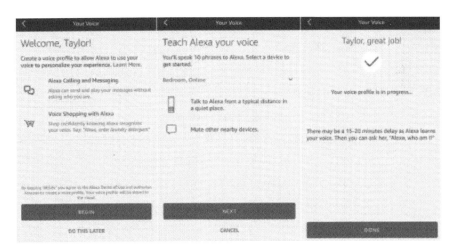

After your training has been completed she will occasionally provide personal results for you. These may include preferences include things like music or information preferences. With this feature enabled you will no longer need to specify who you are for certain skills and applications. This can include functions like receiving messages.

Voice profiles on your device are not permanent and can be easily erased. This can easily be done through the Alexa mobile application. Once inside of the application, navigate to the settings area and select "Your Voice". Once in your voice area you can select "Edit your voice" or "Forget My Voice. Choosing the forget option will delete your voice profile entirely.

Now that your voice is setup you are ready to start giving Alexa commands.

Customizing Your Amazon Echo Show

Customizing your device allows you to give it personality and make it unique to you. There are several areas which may be customized on your device, these include:

- Customizing the home screen
- Updating the wake word on your device
- Customizing shopping preferences
- Updating display settings

Changing Alexa's Wake Word

By default, when speaking to Alexa her default wake word is "Alexa". However, this word can be changed in your device settings. This can be changed to options which include Echo, Amazon or even Computer. To begin swipe downward on your screen and select "Settings". From there tap Device options > Wake word > and select the word which you would like to use.

Adding a Background Photo to Your Device

Another area which can be customized on your device is the background photo. A single photo can be used or alternatively an album can be used for your background. To begin changing your background settings navigate to the Settings. Select Device and tap "Choose a photo". You can select from stock photos or from photos stored in Prime. If you would like to upload a photo to use, it can be done in through the Alexa app and used on the Echo Show.

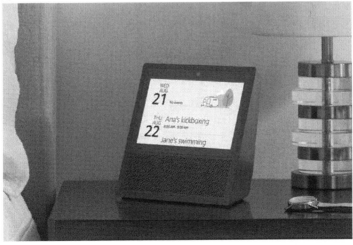

Chapter 2: Creating Routines & Automations with the Echo Show

Routines on the Echo Show

Automation is one thing that your Echo Show makes easier. If you are someone who thrives on a routine, this new feature is perfect for you. Routines allows you to automate tasks in groups. The groups can be created based on times and/or days of the week. For example, if you wake up at the same time every day you can create a routine to turn on the lights at a specific time each day.

Routines can be created from within the Alexa app. From the menu select Routines and select the plus sign to create a new one. Select the "When this Happens" button to begin. This will allow you to choose the trigger for your action. Select add action and select the device which will be altered by this action.

Deleting routines can be done in a similar way. However instead of selecting the + you will need to select the routine which you would like to delete. After selecting the desired routine choose menu and select "Delete Routine" to remove it.

Scheduled Tasks

Are you someone who needs constant reminders and notifications when things need to be done? Alexa now allows you to create scheduled and recurring reminders using your voice. For example, "Alexa, remind me to [walk the dog] every [Saturday] at [8 PM]. On your Echo Show, when the reminder sounds you will be shown the reminder text and it will remain on the screen until you have dismissed it.

Reminders can also be managed within the Alexa application. Simply navigate to Reminders & Alarms. Select the device you would like to set or alter the reminders for from the dropdown menu. Open the reminders tab to view the status of current reminders or to create more. To see reminders which have already been completed, select "Completed Reminders".

Alarms perform much like the reminders. They can be set for a later date or for the same day. You can have up to 100 timers or alarms at one time. It is important to remember that Do not disturb will not block timers or alarms. If your device has been muted or is not connected to Wi-Fi, your timers and alarms will still sound.

You can now even set your alarms to sound to certain music or playlists. This music must be available through one of the following sources:

- Amazon Music
- iHeartRadio
- Spotify (paid subscriber)
- TuneIn
- Pandora

When attempting to set an alarm using music simply tell Alexa, "Alexa, wake me up to Beyoncé". Your device will use your default music option to play music from.

Chapter 3: Getting the Most out of Alexa

If you didn't already know, Alexa skills are the bread and butter of mainly all Amazon Echo device systems. Skills are programs or entities which are designed to help you perform a variety of basic and complex functions. These skills can be for things like recipes, workouts or even games.

The Echo Show not only can perform the voice activated functions, it can also provide you with supplemental information on the screen. For example, when using skills like Uber you will see your driver's time of arrival on your screen.

You even can enable skills from your mobile phone or via voice through the device itself. To begin enabling skills through Alexa you must know the name of the skill which you would like to activate. This can be done by simply saying, "Alexa, enable [skill y]". The skill will now be available for you to use form then on.

There are several skills which work exceptionally well with your device. These skills utilize voice and screen.

1. **Fandango:** This skill allows you to not only watch the latest movie trailers but also connect to your personal fandango account. Connecting your account allows you to not only stay up to date with your favorites but also see information about movie show times from your home theater. Now you don't have to rely on Alexa to tell you everything. You can see it for yourself on the screen. You can even purchase tickets.

2. **Uber**: Using the Uber skill on your device allows you to see arrival times as well as offering the ability to pick your car service. You won't need to look at your phone again when you have the Echo Show around.

3. **Openable**: Open Table allows you to plan the perfect date night without having to lift a finger. This skill allows you to make reservations on the fly right from your device. Your screen allows you the ability to search for the perfect restaurant and plan to make it a reality.

4. **Jeopardy**: If you are looking for something to play that's fun and can keep everyone entertained, look no further. The Jeopardy skill is perfect for any family night. Watch the

clues as they come across your display and even see statistics on how well you are doing in the game.

5. **Food Network:** Do you often find yourself looking for recipes on the fly? Are you someone who loves to cook and try new things? Food Network is the perfect skill. You no longer must listen for Alexa's voice when working through instructions. They are displayed on your screen and provide you with the ability to stop and start as needed. If you are looking for more surrounding the channel, she can even show you what is currently playing.

6. **Shopping:** If you are looking for specific products and your local grocery store may not have them, ask Alexa. Simply say, "Alexa Scan". This will allow you to scan the barcode of the item you are looking for and see the

product or similar products on Amazon's website.

7. **Ring**: The Ring Camera allows you to integrate your Alexa device with your home. This camera is placed at your front door and lets you see just who is visiting. Screening visitors has never been easier. No more tip toing to the window for a peek.

Did you know you can even ask Alexa questions? These questions can range from weather information to even recipes. The list blow provides you with sample questions that Alexa can answer without utilizing a skill.

- Alexa, what time is it?
- Alexa, what is the weather in [insert city here]?
- Alexa, can you find me a dumpling recipe?
- Alexa, why do we celebrate Easter?
- Alexa, does Santa Claus exist?
- Alexa, when is Christmas?
- Alexa, how many teaspoons in a tablespoon?

Aside from these questions Alexa can also provide information surrounding various holidays and major events. You can find out what these skills are bye simply asking "Alexa, what holiday skills do you have?"

To get started with using skills they must be enabled. This can be done from the Alexa application or from your personal computer.

Enabling Skills on the Echo Show

If you are enabling skills from your home computer, simply navigate to www.amazon.com/skills. You will need to log into the name which corresponds to your Alexa Account. Once on the site, use the search feature or category bars to find skills which corresponding to your needs and lifestyle. Finally, after finding a skill which meets your needs simply tap "enable".

When enabling skills, it is important to remember that some skills will require additional information, accounts or even subscriptions to be fully integrated with your device.

When using your Echo Show device simply ask Alexa to open a skill or enable a skill. If supplemental information is needed, you will be asked to refer to the Alexa application.

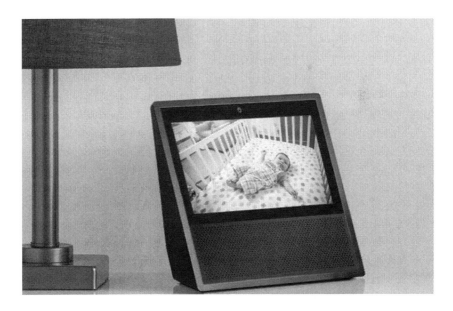

Managing Your Enabled Skills

This section will cover the deletion of skills and how to remove them from your account.

To begin viewing and changing your skills you must open the Alexa application. The Alexa application is the hub for her management. From your menu accordion select "Skills" and then Select "Your Skills". This will show you all your skills. Once here you can alter any of the listed skills.

The following functions are available upon selection of a single skill.

1. Disable Skill – Use this function when you no longer need a skill and would like to make it inactive. Press the disable button within the application or command Alexa to disable it. Please remember that disabling a skill does not delete a potentially corresponding account on the vendor's site.

2. Notifications – Not all skills have notifications. However, this controls if you would like to turn them off if a skill does have them.

3. Review – Reviewing a skill allows you to provide your opinion of the skill for other Amazon users to see. This is one feature that cannot be done via Alexa. Tap the "Write a Review" option within any skill to begin reviewing skills.

4. Provide permissions for Children's skills – These skills determine if this is something which is available to a children's profile. Detailed permissions are handled within the parent consent area.

5. Managing Permissions for Skills – This option allows you to manage what items on your device the skill has access to. These are generally given when an item is downloaded and used. However, if your trust in the skill is uncertain, these can be taken away.

Although the screen is a great addition to the Echo Show, it is still uncommon. This was Amazon's first device to include a camera and a display. This means that many skills may not have a display interface.

Fun with Your Amazon Echo

There are multitude of functions you can do with the Alexa device. These include playing games, asking trivia questions and receiving a variety of information. The list below includes information for experimenting with your Amazon Echo Show.

- *Discovering New Music*: Use your device to discover new and interesting music with

Alexa. She can not only tell you what's popular she can also find new music. Suggested commands include – "What's popular with Beyoncé?"

- *Play Games with Your Device*: Use your device to have some fun by asking Alexa to play a game or tell a few jokes. Suggested commands include: "Alexa, sing a song." "Alexa, tell me a joke." "Alexa, play rock, paper, scissors."
- *Podcasts & Radio* – Use Alexa to play your podcasts and radio shows. These items will come from iHeartRadio and TuneIn. Suggested commands include: "Alexa, play The Read Podcast."
- *Movies in Your Area* – Alexa can also help you discover what movies and movie trailers are playing near you. Suggested commands include: "Alexa, show the trailer for Star Wars." "Alexa, what movies are playing near me?"
- *Music Lyrics* – Have you ever been searching for your music lyrics and just couldn't find them? Suggested commands include: "Alexa, show the lyrics."
- *Basic Information*: Alexa is also able to provide material for a variety of basic information. This will include information on basic measurements, recipes, conversions, tips, advice and much more. Suggested commands include: "Alexa, how many ounces are in 20 lbs.?" "Alexa, what is 2 +9?" "Alexa, how do you spell donut?"

Traffic Information: Based on the address information for home and work in your account you can receive traffic and commute updates. Suggested commands include: "Alexa, what's my commute."

Chapter 4: Media on the Echo Show

Your Echo show is a big powerhouse in a small shell. It comes equipped with video and photo capability using the attached camera. This chapter will give your insight into what you can do with your photos, creating slideshows and using the photo booth.

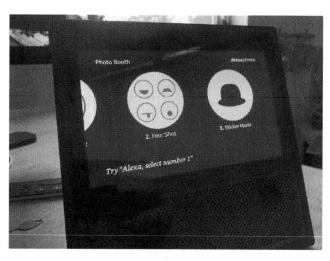

Echo Show Photo Booth

Your photo booth can be compared to that which you would find on your MacBook or an iPhone. This feature allows you to take multiple pictures of different fun types. There are 3 different types of pictures. These include Single Shot Photography, 4 shot photography or sticker mode. Any photos taken in any of these modes are automatically uploaded to Prime Photos and available for use within your slideshow.

When attempting to take a photo simply tell Alexa what type of photo you would like to take. You can either tell her to take your picture or take a picture of another type.

Commands Associated with your Echo Show Camera

Alexa can aid you in finding pictures based on a variety of metadata. This can include album name or even day. Use the following commands in when using your Echo Show Camera.

Searching Images on the Echo Show

These commands correspond to items when being grouped by date

"Alexa, display pictures from [Easter 2017]"

"Alexa, display pictures from [Thanksgiving]"

"Alexa, show me pictures from [Sasha's birthday]"

"Alexa, show me what's in my Family Vault."

"Alexa, show me what's in my Family Vault."

You also can search images on your Echo Show. These can be found by event name, location or even person. Use the commands below to begin searching through Alexa.

"Alexa, show me pictures of Emma."
"Alexa, show me pictures from Chicago."
"Alexa, show me pictures from Blue Concert"

Changing your Slideshow

The Echo Show provides the ability for your slideshow to be updated via voice or via the touch screen on your device.

Use the following commands to update your slideshow using your voice:

"Alexa, go to the next photo."
"Alexa, turn on shuffle."
"Alexa, pause the slideshow."
"Alexa, resume my slideshow."

"Alexa, turn on shuffle mode."
"Alexa, please go to the prior photo."

Your slideshow can also be manipulated via the device itself.

To begin making changes from your device swipe downward on your Echo Show screen and select "Settings". From there select "Display" and select "Photo Slideshow".

From here you can change the speed of the slideshow as well as set your playback preferences.

Chapter 5: Shopping with the Amazon Echo Show

Shopping is a major function of the Amazon Echo Show device. Unlike the other Echo devices, the Echo Show provides a way for users to see what exactly they are ordering. To begin purchasing via voice you must follow a few short instructions to set it up.

How to Set Up Voice Purchasing

Voice purchasing provides a way for users to repurchase items they have purchased in the past. Amazon also provides promotional pricing for various items purchased via voice purchasing. When you first utilize your Echo Show, voice purchasing will be enabled by default. If you are attempting to alter your Voice Purchasing settings, this will need to be done in the Alexa mobile application.

Navigate to the settings within the application. Locate the Accounts button and select it. Once in this area select Voice Purchasing. Here you will have the ability to toggle voice purchasing on or off. Your 1 Click payment settings can also be altered from this area – select "Vie Payment Settings to begin doing so.

Your Voice Purchasing Code

Using a voice code secures your ability to make voice purchases and stops anyone from making them on your account. Voice codes are 4-digit pin numbers which are used to confirm and complete purchases made via your Alexa device. Voice codes can be turned on or off from within the application settings. You can create and confirm you code in your mobile device. If you have already set up a voice profile Alexa can be used to distinguish your voice when making purchases. This function will also need to be turned on in the app settings.

To do so toggle the switch which reads "Allow recognized speakers to purchase without the voice code after giving it just once". After toggling this setting, you will only be asked for the code on your first purchase. Ever subsequent purchase will utilize voice recognition for determining if you are the individual placing the order. Once this feature is no longer active, your device will use the Voice Code option to determine if it should ask for a code when purchasing.

Creating & Managing Lists on the Echo Show

Have you ever had to jot down a note on the back of a piece of mail just so you don't forget? Now, Alexa is at your rescue. Alexa allows you to not only create to do lists but shopping lists as well. Once these lists are created they can be accessed from within the Alexa application, the Amazon website and even your other Alexa devices.

Lists can be created directly from the mobile application, website or via Alexa. To create a list simply say, "Alexa, create a to-do list/shopping list". After your list has been created you can then begin to add items to it. Your list cannot exceed 100 items and the maximum character count for titles are 256 characters.

After your list is created you may tell Alexa things like, "Alexa – add toothpaste to my shopping list".

Dash Buttons – Virtual

If you are not familiar with Virtual Dash buttons they are the perfect way to never miss an item again. If you are familiar with physical dash buttons you will know that when push they create orders for specific products. The virtual dash buttons operate in a similar manner except they cannot be physically pushed. Using your Echo Show's screen, Alexa can show you what virtual dash buttons you currently have. You can scroll through this list as and check for what items you currently have. There are several virtual dash buttons each equipped with a corresponding product. Your virtual dash buttons can also be accessed through the application or the Amazon website. These buttons are exclusively for Amazon Prime.

After you have found the item which you are attempting to purchase simply say "Alexa, buy this". Once you have confirmed via voice or via the on-screen prompts that your order is correct you will receive the order confirmation number and an estimated delivery date.

Using your dash buttons is simple and easy if 1 click payment is enabled on your device with a valid shipping address. If it is not, you will not be able to use this service.

Prime Now

Did you know that you could use Prime Now with your Alexa device? Prime Now allows select orders to be delivered right to your doorstep within a 2-hour span. If you need an item right away, prime now is the option for you. Prime now allows users to receive everyday day items like Kleenex, toilet paper and even snacks. This also includes restaurant delivery. However, restaurant delivery is only available in select cities. If your city does not appear on the list below it is not available in your city yet.

- San Diego (California)
- Austin (Texas)
- Baltimore (Maryland)
- Minneapolis (Minnesota)
- Tampa (Florida)
- Orlando (Florida)
- Northern Virginia)
- Portland, OR.
- Atlanta, (Georgia
- Manhattan (New York)
- Brooklyn (New York)
- Seattle (Washington)
- Dallas (Texas)
- San Francisco (California)
- San Jose (California)
- Oakland (California)
- Los Angeles (California)
- Orange County (California)
- Chicago (Illinois)
- Washington, D.C.
- Phoenix (Arizona)
- Columbus (Ohio)
- Las Vegas (Nevada
- Houston (Texas)

- Miami (Florida)

To begin ordering with Prime Now, all you must do is specify this when attempting to purchase an item with Alexa. For example, say things like "Alexa order Doritos from Prime Now". After she searches through the Prime Now Catalog, Alexa will confirm the item information with you. Once you confirm its validity she will provide you with the confirmation.
There are some stipulations when ordering through Alexa with Prime Now. Your order must not be below the minimum order value. When your order does not surpass this threshold, she will provide options for items which will increase your order total.

When using Prime Now you must specifically specify this with Alexa or else your order will be placed normally. It is also important to remember that if an item is not offered through Prim Now but is offered through the regular Amazon Store, she will not tell you.

Please remember that when making purchases via Prime Now any items in your online cart will not be moved or transferred to your prime now cart. Alexa also cannot provide any updates on previously placed Prime Now orders. In order to receive status information, you will need to use the Prime Now website or the Prime Now mobile app. Currently, Alexa cannot alter Prime Now orders delivery hours. Any tips or donations to your Prime Now delivery person will also need to be done via the Prime Now Application and not Alexa.

Amazon Restaurants

Along with ordering things via Prime Now, Alexa also provides the ability to reorder your favorite meals from your favorite restaurants. This feature is available for user who hold a Prime Membership. You must also have had 1 meal ordered in the past.

To use Amazon restaurant the Amazon Restaurants skill must be enabled. If it is not simply say, "Alexa, enable the Amazon Restaurants skill". This can also be done via the mobile application.

Once the application is enabled, Alexa will aid you in ordering past meals from various restaurants. Once your order has been placed they can be easily tracked through the Prime Now application.

When completing ordinary orders on your Echo Show all you must do is tell Alexa what it is you are looking to order. Once she has received your request Alexa will show you the top-rated items on the screen. You can manually swipe through the listed items or use Alexa to purchase or show more options. You will then be taken through a series of steps to complete your order.

It wouldn't be right if you weren't able to purchase Amazon Echo devices through Alexa. When beginning with your initial Echo order simply tell Alex, "Alexa, I want to order 2 Echo Looks". For some items, Alexa has a limit however if the order is eligible se will continue with prompts. After she has found the item you are requesting you will have the option to confirm your purchase or cancel it. Once it has been placed it can be found in the orders section of your Amazon account. You can also ask Alexa for occasional updates.

Chapter 6: Drop In, Voice Messaging & Calling

The new Drop In feature of Alexa allows you to drop into any Echo Device and use it like an intercom. This feature is only usable with certain Amazon devices, these include:

- Echo Dot
- Amazon Echo

- Echo Plus
- Echo Spot
- Echo Show

Although Drop In is available on these devices, it must first be enabled. To enable and use Drop In you must be signed up "Alexa Calling & Messaging". This is a feature which can be toggled through the Alexa enabled.

The Alexa Calling & Messaging service allows user to call other Echo devices. Alexa can make 3 types of calls: Alexa to Alexa, Calling, Alexa to Alexa Messaging and calls to mobile or land line numbers. Mobile or landline numbers must be from U.S, Canada or Mexico. There is no international calling, as of yet.

To begin signing up for this service, navigate to the Alexa application. Any users in your phone who are using a connected Echo device will be added to your Alexa Contacts. After you have completed sign up and your contacts have been synced, you must choose at least one contact you would like to use Drop In with. For you to drop in on them, they must enable you for drop in from their contacts list. This is not something which you can do, however, it must be done before the service can be used.

Once these steps have been completed, you can begin to use Drop In.

Managing Your Messaging & Calling Profile

Your messaging profile can be managed through the Alexa Application. This is managed through the conversations tab on your home page. From the contacts icon within conversations, select the "My Profile" option. You will then have the option to update a variety of information surrounding your profile. This includes your name, drop in settings and caller ID. Your drop-in setting is used to determine if you can drop in on others and devices within your home. Your Caller ID can also be turned off or on. This setting will determine if your mobile name and number will be displayed when calling land lines.

Managing Your Drop-in Permissions

To successfully use Drop In permissions for the device must be turned on. These permissions are what controls your ability to drop in. To alter permissions, use the steps below:

A. Navigate to the Conversation area of the Amazon Alexa application by selecting the messaging icon from the home screen of your app. Select the contact icon in the top right hand corner of the screen. This is the person icon.
B. Navigate to the contact which you would like to alter and select their name.
C. Toggle the button on the user's contact record for Drop In. This will allow or block permissions on the contact.

D. Drop Ins can also be done on your own devices; however, they must first be enabled on your profile.

The Amazon Echo Show allows users to place video calls to anyone who owns an Echo Show or other Echo device with messaging capabilities. To begin a call simply say, "Alexa, call [Ashley]". To begin a call the recipient must be in the contact list. When on a call, your video can be toggled on or off.

How to Make Calls with the Echo Show

To begin a call using your Echo Show simply give Alexa the following command: "Alexa, Call [Brody]". If there are multiple options under one contact you can specify which is the default. You also have the option to speak the full number to Alexa.

The commands below show you how to place calls using your Echo device:

- Dial an Echo device – "Alexa, call (Alice)".

- End a call – "Alexa, [End call]/ [hang up the call].

- Dial a number – "Alexa, "Call 7-0-8-3-4-2-4-5-6-3

- Mute Call – To mute a call simply use the microphone button on your Echo.

Chapter 7: Using Your Echo Show with Home Cameras

Even with a screen Alexa can still be the hub for all your smart home devices. This includes things like lighting, cameras and even home appliance. Your Echo show makes things even simpler with the use of its display. With items like the Ring Camera for your front door or even baby monitoring software, you can now view camera feeds directly on your Echo Show.

With your Echo Show you get much of the same functionality that is available through your regular sized Amazon Echo, with the bonus of having the screen.

Setting Up Your Camera Device

Setting up your camera feed on your Amazon Echo is fairly quick and easy. Once you have purchased a compatible camera navigate to the skills section of the Alexa application and search for the skill which corresponds to your camera. Follow the given prompt in order to link the two devices together. Once you have enabled the skill you will need to add the device itself within Alexa. This can be done by Selecting Add Device. This will allow Alexa to find your camera. After your device is found it will now be listed under Devices in the Alexa app.

To begin showing or hiding your camera feed simply ask Alexa to show you a specific feed. This will open the camera view on your device.

Chapter 8: The Echo Show: The Nucleus of Your Smart Home

With your Echo Show you can not only control your camera feeds you can also control things like lighting, sprinklers, garages, TVs and even fans. You even have the power to schedule various functions to happen at certain times. Your device will work with a variety of brands like WeMo, Ring, Arlo, Hue and wink.

Connecting Smart Home Devices to Alexa

To begin connecting devices ensure that your device is connected to your Wi-Fi network and that you have followed the instructions with the manufacturer. Once that is completed, navigate to the skills menu and enable the skill which corresponds to the device and follow the on-screen instructions. To begin discovering devices simply tell Alexa to discover my devices.

Using Hubs with Your Echo Show

When using hubs, you can connect the hub to your Echo and control a number of other devices. These hubs allow you to create scenes, manage entertainment hubs and control lighting. Some devices need hubs in order to operate with the Echo Show or any other Alexa enabled devices. These are devices which do not have Alexa skills.

Compatible Hubs with Alexa devices include:

- Vivint

- Lutron

- Samsung SmartThings

- Wink

- Insteon

- Nexia

- Securifi Almond

The Harmony Hub is one hub which cannot be set up directly through Alexa or your Echo. In order to work with the device, you must use apps like Yonomi to integrate them with Alexa.

Basic Voice Commands

There are many basic commands which can be used with all Smart Home devices. These are simple universal commands to use with devices. These commands include the following:

Turning Your Device On & Off – Alexa, turn off [device name].

Setting lighting brightness – Alexa, set the brightness to 80%.

Changing your fan speed – Alexa, set the living room fan to [55] %

Locking & Unlocking door – Alexa, lock the [front door].

Alexa, is the [front door] locked?

Advanced Voice Commands to Control Your Smart Devices

If you are looking to go beyond the basics you can even trigger multiple actions with one command. This can happen when using Smart Device Routines. Routines can be created by selecting Routines from the application and selecting the plus sign. Select "When This Happens" and choose how to trigger. You will then need to add an action.

You can also modify or delete routines from within the application.

Using Alexa Smart Groups

Smart groups are a great way to control multiple items at once. Once items are within a group they can be easily controlled with a single command. This functionality can be used for lighting, appliances or in conjunction with many other categories of smart devices. Settings for these groups are managed within the Alexa application from the Smart Home area.

Chapter 9: Creating a Smarter & More Powerful Home

How to Use Yonomi with Alexa

Yonomi is an app which allows you to trigger routines using Alexa. It can directly be compared to IFTTT. Outside of the routines which Alexa controls, you can turn on or off single devices using Yonomi. These can include turning on or off Apple TV, Sonos players, WeMo or Quirky devices. Yonomi also provides a wider range of connectable devices than IFTTT, although it does not come with an interface which is as fancy.

Yonomi provides the ability to create a long string of actions which may be tedious to set up but rewarding in the end.

In order to set up the Yonomi skill find the skill in the Smart Home area of the Alexa application. Once found select to Enable the skill. Once complete you will need to tell Alexa to discover any new smart home devices.

Your Nest Thermometer & Camera

Your Nest Thermometer is equipped with 2 skills which will allow it to easily work with Alexa. To begin using your device, simply enable one or both skills from the Alexa Application. The two skills are Nest Thermostat by Nest Labs or Nest Camera by Nest.

Controlling the temperature with your Nest Thermometer is extremely easy. Simply use the thermostat name to tell Alexa what you would like to do. For example:

- Alexa, what's the temperature in the [living room]?
- Alexa, increase the temperature in the [bedroom] by 5 degrees.

You also have similar commands for your nest camera.

- Alexa, show the feed from the [baby's room].
- Alexa, show [outside lot] feed.

Using Your Phillips Hue

The Phillips Hue allows you to control color and brightness on your device. You can also create scenes and rooms within your Hue settings. To begin controlling the lights in your home simply connect the Phillips Hue skill with your device. After connecting your device changing the settings is simple.

To change the color of the lights in your home tell Alexa the color you desire and watch it change.

- Alexa, set the bedroom light to red.
- Alexa, make the living room light warmer.

Creating IFTTT Recipes with Alexa

Creating Recipes with IFTTT is easy and can be done for several items. Once you have successfully connected your Alexa device to IFTTT the possibilities are endless. You can connect things to Gmail, social media, outlook, Spotify and many other applications.

Aside from a variety of music applications and services, IFTTT also functions extremely well with Smart Home devices, appliances, lighting and hubs. This allows you to handle the same functions which you would normally handle directly through the Alexa device.

Creating recipes is the main thing you must do in IFTTT. This is where you create the trigger words and phrases which will set off events. IFTTT is used in replacement of the typical Alexa Skill. When using this application, no skills are needed. The following information will show you how to create skills with IFTTT and how to integrate them with your Echo device.

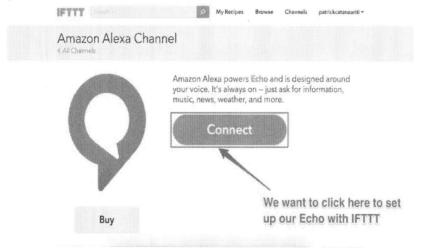

1. To begin using IFTTT you will need to have an active account and be connected using the mobile application or the website. For ease of use, these steps will guide you using the IFTTT website. Once you are on the IFTTT website, navigate to the Alexa page. Here you will need to select the word connect. You will then need to log in using your associated Amazon account. This should be the same account which is connected and used for your Echo Show.

2. After signing in, to continue you will need to acknowledge that you agree to the terms and conditions from the IFTTT screen. Once this is completed, you are now connected.

3. Once you have successfully connected, you will see a list of recipes which have been predefined. These will allow you to use ready-made recipes which you do not need to alter, simply set up. You will also have the option to create new recipes from scratch. The method used within this tutorial can be used universally as a guide to setting up recipes.

To begin, from the top right corner of your screen choose the Create button. Once again you will need to search for the channel which will trigger the activity. This will be the Echo Channel.

Next you will need to choose a trigger for your desired recipe. You will be presented with many options. These will include things like saying a certain phrase or adding an item to a to do list. We will be using the option to say a specific phrase. Once you have chosen the option, you will be prompted to enter your phrase in the text box and choose create trigger.

After you have created the trigger, you will need to find the item which you are attempting to connect the trigger to. This will most times be the brand of the smart device. Simply type in the brand's name to continue.

From there you will need to choose the action associated with the device. This is what will happen when the trigger phrase is spoken. Depending on what action you choose, there will be corresponding options which will need to be set. For example, when turning on a light it would need to know which light, what color to illuminate and so on.

Your recipe is completed once you have reached the confirmation page. Your item is now ready to use.

IFTTT Integration for Music

IFTTT brings a lot of added functionality to your Echo Show. It gives you the ability to connect with applications which you normally wouldn't have the ability. There are several applets for music goers which make IFTTT a great integration for Echo Users.

IFTTT has extensive integration with Spotify, Soundcloud, Genius, Songkick and many more. This allows you to do things like create playlists, get the latest music updates and send social updates on trigger. Did you know you can even create a playlist filled with all the songs played by Alexa on your device? All of this is possible through IFTTT.

Using IFTTT you can find recipes others have created or even start your own from scratch.

When using your device to play music, it is important to remember that a default must be set when provide Alexa with general commands. These are commands which do not specify a skill to use. To set a default, this will need to be done from within the Alexa mobile application.

For example, if using Spotify as your default music option, navigate to the settings within the app and choose Music & Media. From there you will need to link the account of the desired music service. IF this service is Spotify, you will need to log in using your Spotify credentials and choose Default Music Services and select the application. Once this has been linked you can say things like, "Alexa, play Beyoncé". Once this is said it will automictically play a random Beyoncé themed playlist on Spotify.

Using Musixmatch on Your Echo Device

If you are unfamiliar with Musixmatch, it is a skill which helps you learn song lyrics. It can easily be enabled by telling Alexa to enable it or by doing it manually from the Alexa App. Once it is enabled simply say things like "Alexa, get the lyrics for Sorry". You can also give the skill the exact name and title to find the exact song. If you're ever looking for a song based on a specific lyric you can ask the Musixmatch application to find it.

You can even say things like – "Alexa, what song contains the words, if you like it then you should have put a ring on it".

Signul Beacon

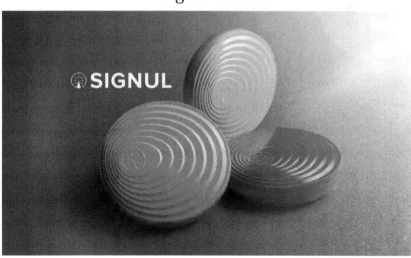

Signul Beacon allows users to create a bridge by detecting when your phone is absent. This application allows users to send messages, control home automations and so much more. Users can define events which can be entry or exit events which trigger certain action and automation. IFTTT now provides integration with Signul Beacon. This allows users to log a spreadsheet, send a tweet, turn your lights on or do a variety of other activities.

Chapter 10: Useful Alexa Commands & Functions

How to Get Help from Alexa

Alexa can help you with several key features and functions. If you are looking to utilize Alexa for help simply say, Alexa help. She can help with connecting to Bluetooth or specific questions. If you are looking for more advanced help with Alexa, navigate to the Help & Feedback section of the Alexa application.

Using Alexa For Basic Calculations

Do you have young children in your home who often need help and assistance with homework? No worries, Alexa can provide that. Out of the box, Alexa comes with the capability to answer a variety of math and conversion functions with. This is just one of the many things that Alexa can do without downloading a skill. In order to begin simply start by saying your wake word and try any one of the commands below:

Basic Math

Multiplication: Alexa, what is 5 x 7?
Division: Alexa, what is 30 divided by 3?
Subtraction: Alexa, what is 20 minus 10?
Addition: Alexa, what is 4 plus 7?

Advanced Math

Aside from the everyday functions listed above, Alexa can even perform advanced math functions. These include things like square roots, pi or roots? Use the list below to guide you in talking with Alexa.

Alexa, what is [7] squared?
Alexa, what is [3] to the power of [4]?
Alexa, what is [3] cubed?
Alexa, what is [9] factorial?
Alexa, what's the value of Pi?
Alexa, what is [25%] of [4565]?
Alexa, what is the square root of [6]?
Alexa, is [2320] a prime number?

Alexa in the Kitchen

Your Echo show can be used nearly anywhere in your home. Placing the Echo Show in your kitchen could be a bigger help than you would have ever imagined. Alexa can aid in increasing your kitchen productivity and even help you come up with recipes. The most useful skills on the kitchen include:

- Creating a grocery list for preparing some of your favorite recipes
- Guiding you step by step through new edible creations.
- Using timers for food preparation and baking
- Converting a variety of different measurements
- Get your morning coffee started before you even get up

If you're cooking and need to double a recipe, what do you do? Do you round up to the nearest measurement that sounds right or do you whip out your calculator? If either one of these applies to you, with Alexa in your kitchen, you never have to do it again. Ask Alexa exactly how much you need and she has it covered. Without any additional skills Alexa can provide general and metric conversions. To get Alexa started with conversions use the phrases below:

- Alexa, how many cups are in a pint?
- Alexa, how many teaspoons equal a tablespoon?

- Alexa, how many teaspoons are in 6 tablespoons?
- Alexa, set a timer for 30 minutes?

Alexa Optimized for the Echo Show

The Echo Show was one of the first devices to offer a touch screen on the device. Not only does it show information when needed pertaining to your questions asked of Alexa, it is also interactive. The show allows you the choice of using your screen, your voice or both to communicate more effectively. There are a few commands which have been optimized to make your Echo Show work with you. There are several commands which trigger screen actions these include but are not limited to the following:

- Alexa, show me my calendar.
- Alexa, show the baby's room camera.
- Alexa, show me the movie trailer for Black Panther.
- Alexa, show me the forecast for this week in Chicago.
- Alexa, show me any outstanding timers.
- Alexa, play my flash briefing.

Getting Local Information Using Alexa

Did you know Alexa can provide you with information on your local businesses and local news? This is out of the box functionality which provides information based on the home address you have listed within the Alexa mobile app or the city which is spoken. Alexa can provide business hours, phone numbers and even restaurant information.

If you're hungry and wondering what's open late, you can always ask Alexa. She can provide several business information like phone numbers, address and even hours. Alexa can also provide you with information on your local news. She is also able to provide travel information.

- Alexa, find me a Chinese restaurant.
- Alexa, how late is Pizza Hut open?
- Alexa, give me business hours for Wal-Mart.
- Alexa, give me today's music flash briefing.
- Alexa, what's in today's news?
- Alexa, what is my commute to work today?

Manage Household Members on Your Device

When using Amazon, you may have multiple adult accounts that can be used with your devices. This allows them to listen to music, share content and access custom information. Household accounts can be easily created within the Alexa application. Please be mindful that the person using the added account will be authorized to use your credit card information. Also on the Echo Show your prime photos will be seen by the other authorized users. However, access may be restricted to certain users.

To create a new account, follow the instructions below:

1. From the mobile application select Settings from the menu.
2. Once in the Settings area select Household Profile from within the Accounts area.
3. Once there follow the instructions on screen and have the user enter in their account information.

Removing a Household Account

Just as easily as you add a household account, it can be removed. However, once a user has been removed you will not bc able to add an account for at least 180 days. Use the information below as a guide to how to remove an account.

1. From inside of the Alexa application select Settings.
2. Once inside navigate to the account section of the page and choose **In an Amazon household with [Person Name]**.
3. Click the Remove button found next to the desired user. You are attempting to remove yourself, simply select Leave.
4. You will need to confirm your choice by selecting Remove again.

Chapter 11: Troubleshooting the Echo Show

If you find yourself having a hard time with your Echo Show there are several ways that you can troubleshoot your device before contacting Amazon.

Restarting Your Device

If your screen becomes unresponsive a restart may help to solve any issues. In order perform the restart, start by unplugging the power adapter from the device. Then plug it back into the Echo Show. Your device should then begin to reboot. You should not restart your device on its initial boot.

Resetting Your Device

If you are looking to give your device to someone else or for any reason you find that your device is not as responsive as you would like, resetting your device may solve your problems. This can be done in the "Settings" area of your device. Swipe downward from the top of your screen and choose settings. Next choose Device options. Here you will see an option to "Reset to Factory Defaults". This will format your device and erase all custom and personal information. Your device will then be back to its day 1 settings and begin the setup process.

Wi-Fi Connectivity Issues

If you are experiencing any issues with your wireless connectivity or intermittent connections use these tips to troubleshoot before contacting Amazon. If your device is having a problem connecting to Wi-Fi networks it will illuminate orange. You can see information related to your Wi-Fi in the settings area under Wi-Fi.

• Attempt to disconnect and reconnect to the wireless network.

• Reduce Wi-Fi Congestion – Congestion may happen when there are multiple devices on your network causing inconsistent connectivity. This can be done in the following ways:

o   Turning off devices which are not in use.

o   Ensure that your devices are not close to product which could interfere with reception. These items would be microwaves or baby monitors.

o   Change the location of your devices to be closer to the router for increased signal strength.

•   Restart your modem or router.

•   Unplug your router or modem. Wait for 30 seconds and plug them back in.

•   Have you recently changed the password to your wireless network? If your Wi-Fi password has been saved to Amazon you will need to save the new password when prompted.

Issues with Alexa Calling

If you find that you are having trouble making and receiving calls with the Alexa Calling services there are several things that you can do to troubleshoot.

The first thing you can attempt to do is check the device. Make sure that you have a compatible device which will allow for Alexa calling. The compatible devices are listed above.

Your Wi-Fi connection is another major component in using the Alexa Calling feature. To ensure that your calls will go through and stay connected, you must have a solid connection.

To begin troubleshooting your Alexa calling start by restarting all your network equipment. This will generally resolve any issues with connectivity. If you are still experiencing issues restart your echo device by unplugging and plugging it back in. If issues continue, you may need to contact your internet service provider for further assistance.

If you find that the issue is not related to your Wi-Fi you may need to check the status of the contact which you are attempting to reach. Check for any spelling issues within your Alexa contacts to ensure that Alexa can understand you. Also, ensure that you are saying the name correctly or not saying anything which may confuse Alexa.

Reminder: Alexa will occasionally check for new contacts or updates to existing contacts to update your Contacts List. If your contact has been recently added, you may need to close and re-open the Alexa application to ensure it has updated. To determine if a contact has been fully updated navigate to the Contacts icon in the Alexa mobile application and check for the updated contact.

If none of these options seem to be working recheck the number which you are intending to call. These numbers can only be U.S, Mexico or Canada.

The following types of numbers cannot be called using your device. These numbers include emergency numbers like 911, toll free numbers or premium rate numbers and abbreviated/information numbers like "211" or "411".

Your last option would be to sign out of the Alexa App. To sign out navigate to the Settings area and select "Sign Out". Once you are prompted, you may sign into the application. This account should be the associated Amazon account for your Echo devices. Start by checking the conversations tab and under the contacts icon to ensure that your contacts are updated and synced.

Conclusion

The Echo show is an extremely versatile and easy to use device. The camera and touch screen are two small additions which add a world of possibility. Your Echo Show is ready to go almost right from the box. Whether you are using Drop In, shopping or just listening to your favorite album, the Echo Show has something for everyone.

With Alexa's integration, what more could you ask for? Your device is capable of continuous learning and updates. You don't have to lift a finger to manually update or worry if it is running the latest software. There are skills for virtually everything you could imagine. Do you need a workout buddy? Are you looking for a chef to aid you with tonight's dinner? Are you looking to keep your busy children entertained? The Echo Show offers these things and more. The only thing left for you to do is learn and discover.

Your device can fit in virtually any environment and it is ready whenever you are. The Echo show provides an unmatched experience.

I hope that this book has proven to be helpful an informative. I also hope that it has made your journey with your new device easier. The Echo Show and Amazon's suite of personal voice assistants continues to grow and change every day. It can only go up from here.

Thanks for reading. I hope you enjoy it. I ask you to leave your honest feedback.

I think next books will also be interesting for you:

Alexa

Amazon Echo

Amazon Echo Guide

Amazon Echo

Amazon Echo Dot

Kindle Fire HD

Kindle Fire HD
8 & 10

The Ultimate User Guide to Master Your Kindle Fire HD

Alex Cooper

Made in the USA
Columbia, SC
03 June 2018